Andalusia

Editorial Everest would like to thank you for purchasing this book. It has been created by an extensive and complete publishing team made up of photographers, illustrators and authors specialised in the field of tourism, together with our modern cartography department. Everest guarantees that the contents of this work were completely up to date at the time of going to press, and we would like to invite you to send us any information that helps us to improve our publications, so that we may always offer QUALITY TOURISM.

QUALITY TOURISM WITH EVEREST

Please send your comments to:
Editorial Everest. Dpto. de Turismo
Apartado 339 – 24080 León (Spain)
Or e-mail them to us at turismo@everest.es

Editorial Management: Raquel López Varela

Editorial coordination: Eva María Fernández and Esteban González

Text: Fernando Olmedo

Photographs: J. M. Gutiérrez, Juan José Pascual, Miguel Raurich, Paolo Tiengo
and Archivo Everest

Diagrams: Mercedes Fernández

Cover design: Alfredo Anievas

Digital image processing: David Aller

Translation: EURO:TEXT, S. L. (Deborah Powell)

Carretera León-La Coruña, km 5 – LEÓN
ISBN: 84-241-0169-3
Legal deposit: LE. 748-2001
Printed in Spain

EDITORIAL EVERGRÁFICAS, S. L.
Carretera León-La Coruña, km 5
LEÓN (Spain)

The bewitching beauty and variety of the Andalusian countryside.

INTRODUCTION

And to the South, Andalusia, the most fascinating of Spanish region that occupies a privileged position at the crossroads between seas and continents at the southern end of the Iberian Peninsula, between the Mediterranean and Atlantic, Europe and Africa, between the Old and New World. If this exceptional situation has meant that it has been a meeting point and cradle for civilisations, which have endowed it with unusual historical wealth and depth, its attractive geographical position has also substantially contributed to its extraordinary power of seduction. The mere mention of Andalusia has awoken the imagination and desire from the earliest times.

It is no accident that numerous traces of its ancestors have been found buried in its ground. The pre-historical traces lead from the daybreak of evolution to the splendour of the legendary *Tartessian* kingdom. The Garden of the Hesperides, where Hercules placed the columns that marked the end of the old world, was located in its hospitable lands. The Betica province, whose goods and men played such an important role in the raising of Rome, covered its generous countryside. The heart of *al-Andalus,* the Hispano-Musulman state which would write one of the most brilliant pages in Medieval western history and the Islamic culture. Its mark on the region was so indelible that it even inherited its name.

Always considered an important area, Andalusia's role became even more significant when it led to the discovery and colonisation of America. Finally, from the end of the 19th century, the predecessors of present-day tourism portrayed it as a Romantic paradise as they were captivated by its bewitching charm, which was an indication of how important it would become as a travel destination.

Festivals, arts and crafts reflect the many facets of this people.

The spectacular human and cultural compendium that defines Andalusia's special features are set against an equally magnificent geographical framework. With around seven and a half million inhabitants and covering an area of 87,268 km^2, it is the most populated autonomous region in Spain and the second largest in terms of area, making it similar in size to countries such as Portugal or Austria. Its very different physical features clearly set it apart from the rest of the peninsular. Sierra Morena's ancient slopes, the escarpment of the Castilian plateau, form its northern edge. The River Guadalquiver, Andalusia's most important river and the region's essential artery, flows for 657 km along this wide valley running from east to west at the foot of the escarpment. To the south of this stretch of cultivated land, another mountain barrier rises up which separates the inland region from the Mediterranean sea. This is the Betic Range, which can be divided up into two basic units: the Sub-Betic mountain range, which runs from the east of Andalusia to the Straits of Gibraltar, and the Penibetic mountain range, the huge geological giant crowned by Sierra Nevada where the highest peak on the peninsular, Mulhancén, rises up to 3,482 m. This map of contrasts, which ranges from Alpine peaks to huge plains and marshlands, is bordered by a long coastline that is also full of contrasts. The Mediterranean coastline is characterised by a rocky landscape, while long beaches of golden sand run alongside the Atlantic.

In harmony with these symbolic features, Andalusia enjoys the mild and favourable climate of the warm southern latitudes, with average annual temperatures of between 16 °C and 18 °C, with mild winters and hot summers and moderate rainfall in autumn and winter. The wide range of different geographical features means that there are many nuances and it is therefore possible to find areas where it snows, next to sub-tropical redoubts or arid desert zones all within a short radius.

Against this background, with three thousand years of history behind it, Andalusia today offers a many-sided panorama where past and present meet, when natural settings go hand in hand with manmade ones. Its secret most probably comes from this subtle synthesis of character. National parks such as the Doñana and Sierra Nevada, protected areas that account for nearly

For a real Andalusian eating, there is a wide array of tapas to choose from.

20% of the region, magnificent monuments such as the Alhambra in Granada, the Mezquita (Great Mosque) in Cordoba or the Giralda tower in Seville and many areas of historical and artistic value which act as backdrops for displays such as Semana Santa (Holy Week), festivities and pilgrimages, with the deep-rooted tradition of flamenco music, with a wide range of craft products, where the healthy Mediterranean diet is the essential part of its gastronomy, which uses excellent natural products –top-class olive oil, fish, vegetables, meats,...– with the added ingredient of the knowledge passed down through the years. All of this is rounded off by the hospitality of a cheerful and open society, and also with the liveliness, the dynamics and the modernity of its capitals, the Costa del Sol and many other spots spread over the eight Andalusian provinces and which ensure the visitor of an unforgettable stay. After discovering Andalusia, more than one person will wonder where they need to go to find more.

Panoramic view of Almería with the Alcazaba and the port.

Almería. Playa del Zapillo. ▶

ALMERÍA

Dawn in Andalusia begins in Almería, which is the most easterly region, and not only due to its place on the map, but also due to its nature and character. Quite rightly, its symbol is the star, outlined as an arch over the schematic human figure of the Indalo or carved in the stone of its Cathedral. Submerged in a secular oblivion, passed over due to the isolation caused by an inadequate communications system and the economic backwardness up to a few decades ago, which has now been renewed thanks to its growing early crops and its enviable tourist attractions, Almería has today emerged out of the great unknown and can be considered a true discovery.

A province with mountains and sea, it can be considered the most Mediterranean of the Andalusian provinces. The deep blue of the waters, the dazzling sky, the majestic landscapes, its popular geometrical architecture reflect the atmosphere to be found along the banks of the *Mare Nostrum,* which emphasises its historical past. Metallurgy was introduced to the Peninsular through here by the peoples from the opposite end of the Mediterranean, according to the evidence provided by the Los Millares and El Argar settlements, while Almería, whose Arabic name means "mirror of the sea", was the main trading point during the Moorish period between *al-Andalus* and the Islam world. A past distilled in a heavy aroma of the East that still floats in the atmosphere.

Two views of the Alcazaba. Below, the Alcazaba and its courtyard.

The Portocarrero Sun, carved on the side walls of Almería Cathedral.

Below: Cabo de Gata. Las Sirenas Cliffs.

The capital, which one writer once described as the most "African" of Spanish cities due to the exotic picture it portrays, is a perfect summary of the province's mood. It is situated at the end of a golf, decorated with rocky outcrops and dominated by the silhouette of the **Alcazaba,** the fortress that Abderraman III ordered to be built in the 10th century. This marked the town being founded and it would continue to spread until after the Catholic Monarchs had taken it in 1489. Its bastion, gardens and palace remains provide a real lesson in history. Below it, the cubic houses, painted in bright colours, are jammed together in neighbourhoods such as La Chanca (the cave quarter), which has caught the attention of artists and writers. Further down, the old part of city stretches to the port and

the Renaissance cathedral, which is the outstanding monument amongst the intimist maze of streets and small squares. The Purchena Gate, the modern centre, reveals a more recent and spacious city, built from the profits of mineral and fruit exports since the 19th century and which left a legacy of modernist buildings in the middle of the encircling contemporary urbanism.
Close to the capital, landscapes and villages provide proof of the area's different personality. First of all, there is **Cabo de Gata,** the fantastic natural park that was formed by volcanic eruptions, with basaltic formations that cut through the cliffs, coves and beaches to the seabed below the crystal-clear waters. A trail of fishing villages, such as **San José** or **Agua Amarga,** are scattered along the coast to the cosmopolitan and tourist enclave of **Mojácar** and the Levante region. Beyond it is the uncultivated land of **Campo de Níjar,** dotted with white villages and towns, and the only desert to be

Cabo de Gata Lighthouse.

Playa de Mojácar.

Above and right, parish church and street in Níjar.
Below, country estate in El Campo de Níjar.

Above, view of Sorbas. Below, Tabernas desert.

found in Europe, the **Tabernas** desert, an area of extreme dryness with a lunar landscape scarred by ravines and gullies. Its dramatic features have been immortalised in films as its has been used as the backdrop for numerous westerns.
The beaches of Aguadulce and the very old **Adra,** from where the last Moorish king of Granada sailed off to exile, are located towards the municipal district of Poniente. The "sea of plastic" from the greenhouses that provide vegetables to half of Europe are to be found around **El Ejido.** The Sierra de Gádor dominates inland, where **Berja** and the River Andarax region are located, together with the beautiful Alpujarra at the end of the foothills of Sierra Nevada. Another group of mountains stands in the centre of the province: the Filabres mountain

Views of Mini Hollywood in Tabernas.

View of Gérgal, in the Filabres mountain range.

range, where villages made up of unusual black-stone buildings nestle amongst its foothills. The River Almanzora valley separates the Filabres from the Estancias and forms a line that runs through **Albox, Cuevas** and **Huércal Overa,** a furrow eroded by the quarrying of the famous **Macael** marbles that were used in the building of the Alhambra and many other monuments. The northern vertex of Almería is finished by the Vélez mountain spur, which penetrates as a cradle into Murcia and La Mancha. Closeby are **Vélez Rubio** and **Vélez Blanco,** which greets the traveller from a haughty peak crowned by its impressive Renaissance castle.

Vélez Blanco, at the foot of the Renaissance castle.

CADIZ

Limestone mountains with steep drops and leafy slopes, forests, meadows and pastures where fighting bulls graze, olive groves and corn fields around dazzling-white villages, dry white land planted with vines, a windswept coast made up of very fine sands, witty people with unequalled artistry, a capital where the oceans waves break against its shoreline like a boat in a fable, and the light, so strong that its heightens the colours and dazzles the visitor's eyes, this is just a glance of what the province of Cadiz has to offer.

The city of Cadiz is an exceptional case: the only island capital to be found on the Peninsula, and the oldest city in the Western world, founded by the Phoenicians 1,100 years before our era. The reason for settling there was due to its relationship with the Atlantic, to which it owes everything, as it acted as a trading post at the edge of the columns of Hercules, that is to say, at the point where the Mediterranean meets the ocean. For centuries, this location made the city wealth and this peaked when America was discovered. Thanks to its bay and its unbeatable location on the route to the Indies, Cadiz became even more important and enjoyed a boom, which marked the course of its history and its delightful appearance for ever, from the 18th century until the colonies won their independence.

Panoramic night-time view of Cadiz.

Town hall and Plaza de San Juan de Dios.

Monument to the 1812 Constitution.

The elegant Cathedral of Cadiz, with its white towers and its sparkling dome made out of golden tiles, dates back to this period, together with Puertas de Tierra (Land Gates), the fortifications that surround the city and the merchants' house with airy watchtowers where they used to stand and watch for the arrival of the fleets. Other details, such as Goya's frescos of the Santa Cueva, dealing with the golden "century of Cadiz", which would end in 1812 with the memorable proclamation of the first Spanish Constitution in the Oratory of San Felipe Neri. Its inhabitants already showed their lack of concern during the siege by the French troops around this time and they softy hummed ballads while the bombs were falling around them, an unusual festive atmosphere that is recalled each year with the most boisterous and lively Carnival that can be experienced.

Phoenician figure in the Archaeological Museum.

Santa Cueva. The Miracle of the Loaves and the Fishes, by Francisco de Goya.

View of the New Cathedral's tiled dome.

The façade of the New Cathedral.

El Puerto de Santa María.
Puerto Sherry.

Main Priory Church
in El Puerto de Santa María.

Sunset over the mouth of the Guadalquivir. ▶

The ports around the Bay are no less delightful and enterprising. The straight streets of **San Fernando** and **Puerto Real** run alongside the aquatic latticework of salt marshes and estuaries. The stateliness of the town centre of **El Puerto de Santa María** standing next to the mouth of the Guadelete under the battlements of the castle of San Marcos, with big rambling houses with large façades and windows with grilles, its outstanding bullring and the fragrance of the wineries, because this is the beginning of the famous land of sherry. The coastal and wine tour continues to **Sanlúcar de Barrameda,** where serene sunsets over the mouth of the Guadalquivir and Doñana can be enjoyed from its noble buildings, livened up the decanting of the invigorating and pale Manzanilla wine.

Arcos de la Frontera. Church of San Pedro above the River Guadalete. ▶

Typical winery in Jerez de la Frontera.

With the appearance of a capital city, **Jerez** is surrounded by vineyards. A place where wine is worshipped, its wineries are as important as the collegiate church of El Salvador and the Alcázar, its most established monuments among a long list of churches and palaces. The city provides a genuine window on life in Andalusia and particularly favours two of its fundamental points: flamenco, which in Jerez is based on the deepest roots of the cante (Andalusian folk music) and the horse, which the Feria (Spring Fair) is dedicated to, carefully bred in the stables that promote and encourage the lineage of the Spanish thoroughbred.
It is worth pausing for the galas held in Jerez's charterhouse before continuing up the Guadalete until reaching one of Spain's most beautiful villages, **Arcos de la Frontera,** a miracle of limestone and stone leaning against a rock carved by a gorge. It has a castle, two churches with cathedral infulae and a captivating urban area that will undoubtedly be stamped on the visitor's memory. Arcos is the starting point

Of all the cities in Spain, Jerez is the most wholeheartedly dedicated to the horse. Jerez hosts the Horse Fair, or Feria del Caballo, and the most brilliant portion of the Fiestas de Otoño (Autumn Fair).

of the route of the white villages in the Cadiz mountain range, with its impressive limestone escarpment and natural park which is home to the remaining rare fir trees, the Spanish Fir, which covers the damp slopes of the Grazalema mountain range. This town and its neighbouring ones –**Zahara** and **Olvera,** vantage points on two large crags, **Setenil,** hidden in a narrow pass, **Ubrique,** which is home to the leather industry– make up a wonderful setting, a place to dream. The province of Cadiz is a triangle that lies between the Mediterranean and Atlantic and marks the extreme southern border of Andalusia and Europe, the southern-most point of the South. **Medina Sidonia** and **Alcalá de los Gazules** overlook the huge pastures where fighting bulls graze and the wood park of Los Alcornocales, **Chiclana, Conil, Vejer,** whose white walls light up the top of a rock, are near to the coast that runs from **Cape Trafalgar** to busy **Algeciras, Gibraltar** and the **Straits of Gibraltar. Tarifa** sticks out into the sea and Africa seems close enough that you can touch it.

La Pastora Arch, in Medina Sidonia.

Medina Sidonia. Star Tower.

Gibraltar seen from La Línea de la Concepción.

Square in Vejer. ▶

Castle of Los Guzmanes, in Tarifa.

Partial view of the old city, with the Roman Bridge and the Mezquita (Great Mosque).

The Mezquita's western façade. ▶

CORDOBA

Few cities can boast of so much antiquity and nobility as Cordoba, which was founded by the Tartessians and Phoenicians, the main centre of the Roman province of *Bética* and capital of the Ommiad caliphate of *al-Andalus,* when it was the most important city in the Western world, an image that remains untouched in this impressive town as we enter the third millennium. The visitor will be struck and enchanted by the view the city provides thanks to its location across the valley at the foot of the brown hills of the Sierra Morena and along the banks of the silver ribbon of the River Guadalquivir, the bastion of Lacalahorra, with the Arab windmills, Felipe II's gate, the Alcázar de los Reyes Cristianos, and the magnificent Mezquita (Great Mosque).

The visitor should first make his way to the temple of sensations that is the **Mezquita,** a World Heritage monument which is incomparable in its genre. It started to be built around the 785 by the first independent emir of *al-Andalus,* Abderraman I, who wanted a splendid building that would last as

Patio de los Naranjos.

The dome of the Mezquita.

Next two pages: Forest of columns in the Mezquita.

proof of his power. His successors, Abdederraman II and III, and, above all Alhaken II, who took the Cordobese caliphate to the height of its splendour, together with prime minister Almanzor, continued the enormous task until the most sumptuous and refined of the Islamic mosques was finished in the 11th century, whose magnificence has left people speechless through the ages. When a room in the Christian style was built in its centre during the 16th century, the emperor Carlos V could only shout at the canons: "you have destroyed something unique to build something common place".

Even from its impenetrable exterior, the Mezquita is a true display of artistic feeling, with delicate façades and decorated with carved marble. The sound of the fountains in the Patio de los Naranjos (Courtyard of the Orange trees) precedes the stillness of the area where Allah was worshiped during six centuries, the astonishing area consisting of a forest of columns and elegant series of bicoloured arches that give the impression of being in a stylised palm grove. The aesthetic feeling vibrates between the harmonious combination of perspectives that culminate in the *mihrab,* the niche looking towards Mecca, lavishly decorated with multi-coloured mosaics.

Following the fantasy of the Mezquita, Cordoba invites the visitor to loose himself and wander through the peaceful streets and along the parapet walks of its old districts where three cultures, Muslim, Hebrew and Christian, co-existed. The synagogue, the Alcázar, the walls and Arab baths, the Bishop's palace, the aristocrats' mansions, the churches and convents that range from the primitive Gothic to the most exuberant Baroque, are the legacy of this extolled mixture. Echoes of Cervantes, of Julio

◀ *Preceding page, inside the Mezquita is the mihrab.*

The combination of searing whitewash and vibrant flowers is the typical style of decoration for Cordovan architecture.

Belalcázar Castle.

◀ *Partial view of the archaeological ruins of Medina Azahara (above); the Salón Rico (Rich Hall) at Medina Azahara (below).*

Romero de Torres, blend with the modern atmosphere and popular customs found in its corners, such as the emblematic squares of El Potro, Las Tendillas or La Corredera. Meanwhile, the sensible rhythm of traditional Cordobese life can be seen in the typical courtyards filled with flowerpots, in the semi-darkness of the taverns where delights of having tapas can be enjoyed, in the silversmith's shops which have turned the city into one of the world leaders in the jewellery sector. In the outskirts, the Palatine city of **Medina Azahara** which the great caliph, Abderraman III dedicated to his beloved adds further to the aura surrounding Cordoba and its region.

The size of the province and its north-south orientation offer a sample of what is to be found in the centre of the region, a cross-section through Andalusia. The plateaux of Los Pedroches and Sierra Morena to the north, with towns under haughty castles, such as **Belalcázar,** and churches made out of hewn stone. The natural parks of Hornachuelos, Cardeña and Montoro protect the wildest side of this landscape, a kingdom of burnt hills with thickets of brushwood and forest which is home to abundant fauna which make it into an area famed for its hunting. At the foot of the mountain spurs winds the green valley of the River Guadalquivir from beautiful **Montoro** to the strong **Almodóvar** fortress.

The ploughed fields of the countryside stretch as far as the eye can see from the river to the south, dotted with wide white villages, pure Andalusia. The vineyards and olive groves churn up the land and break up the landscape and produce the **Montilla region's** famous wines and the excellent virgin oils from **Baena** and **Priego,** towns bursting with history, together with **Aguilar, Lucena, Cabra** and

Above, castle at Almodóvar del Río; left, panoramic view of the fields at Baena; adjoining page, Zuheros Castle.

many others where the healthy produce of the countryside is blended with the extraordinary artistic heritage, so it is not surprising that the south of the province Cordoba is considered as one of the most sublime and original centres of Southern Baroque. The unusual mosaic of people and land in the province of Cordoba reaches its highest point in the limestone crags of the Sub-Betic mountain ranges, which is a splendid natural park dotted with fortified towns, such as **Luque** and **Zuheros,** where the legendary airs of the border romances are still to be found.

Panoramic view of the sea of buildings surrounding the Cathedral in Granada.

GRANADA

Granada's captivating landscape seems to have been designed by a Romantic painter: the fertile Vega del Genil stretches across the foreground and is scattered with a cluster of villages and skirted by a mountain ring, with the white summits of Sierra Nevada floating about the clouds in the background, and in its lap, the capital stands at the foot of the red fort of the Alhambra. Somebody rightly said that the weight of history and art is such in some cities that it transfigures them, transcends their own reality and turns them into a myth. This is what happens in Granada, the city that has had a spell cast over it by the **Alhambra.**

To visit the capital of Eastern Andalusia is to a certain degree to enter in the land of dreams. The visitor has to rub his eyes to believe the rainbow hues that shine at dusk over the walls and towers of the places where the Nazari sultans, the last Muslim kings of Spain, who, during the slow decline of their power, built one of the marvels of the world until they were defeated by the Catholic Kings in 1492. The shady woods and the murmur of the irrigation ditches that surround the monument are a prologue to this fantasy setting. Then the visitor is surprised by the cubist geometry of the towers and doors engraved by the symbol of Islam, the hand that symbolises the five precept of the Koran and the key that opens the way to Eden. Because this is what is hidden behind the walls of the Alhambra, magnificent areas of buildings and gardens that step-by-step keeps in proportion to man, without any pompous perspectives that would overwhelm him. Behind the Renaissance exception of Carlos V's palace the journey through the Nazari

Above, night-time view of the Alhambra. Below, the Alcazaba seen from the Torre de la Vela.

Patio de los Leones.

Royal baths at the Alhambra.

Jardines del Partal. ▶

maze starts the *Mexuar,* with the delicately worked timber, glazed tiles and plasterwork, the placidity of the Alberca courtyard and the Comares palace, the throne room under the canopy of a geometric universe carved in wood, the *Patio de los Leones* (Courtyard of the Lions), the marvellous small wood of columns with rooms embossed with false fretwork, where beams of light shine through, the royal baths, the Partal, nostalgic spaces such as the Cautiva tower, hedges, fountains and the Generalife, the sultans' summer house filled with romances and legends of love affairs.

Panoramic view of the Albayzín, dotted with garden villas or cármenes.

Granada's Moorish patina stretches to the hills that surround the Alhambra. The **Albayzín** district, the heart of the early city, forms a mysterious labyrinth of lanes, slopes and streets that barely widen into small squares in front of the churches that were previously mosques. One example is the Church of El Salvador, the assembly point, which has kept is ancient bathing courtyard, or San Nicolás, at the top of the slope, proving an lookout point over the Alhambra, the old part of the city and the Vega. There are also many old Muslim palaces, such as Dar al-Horra, the sultan's residency, and the famous Granada cármenes, villas with terraced gardens under the shade of sad cypresses. The depth of the local tradition rings out from the craftsmen's workshops and in the flamenco gaiety of the Gypsy dances in the cave district that tunnel into Sacromonte. A more Christian, but no less monumental city spreads over the plain, from the Carrera del Darro and the Plaza Nueva to the huge form of the **Cathedral** and Royal Chapel, an Isabelline Gothic masterpiece that houses the tombs of the Catholic Monarchs and their descendants. The Zacatín, the Alcaicería, the Bibrambla square condense the heart of the traditional life, the hustle and bustle of shops and markets around the official hub of Gran Vía and Puerta Real, milestones of the renovated and modern town that stretches to the banks of the River Genil, the Campo del Triunfo and the monasteries and market gardens in the surrounding areas where the memory of the immortal man from Granada, the poet Federico García Lorca lives on. The splendid majesty of **Sierra Nevada** provides the backdrop. The huge Alpine mountain,

Façade of the Granada Cathedral.

◀ *Local buildings and weaver's shop in Las Alpujarras.*

Typical stew from Las Alpujarras.

Different examples of local arts and crafts from Las Alpujarras.

Slopes and general view of the Sierra Nevada ski station.

which has been declared a national park, marks the roof of the Peninsular stretching between the summits of El Mulhacén and El Veletas, where the most southerly ski slopes in Europe can be enjoyed.
The province goes down from the stark inland high plateau to the mild Costa Tropical. The wild landscapes of **La Sagra,** the region's second highest area, and of **Huéscar,** are to be found up there and then the tortuous landscape of valleys, ravines and the mountain ranges of **Baza** and **Guadix,** both of which have cathedrals, and a fantastic cave district, which defies all town planning and architectural convention, form part of the second town. The charming small villages of the Marquesado del Cenete dominated by the Renaissance feats of **Lacalahorra** castle seem stranded in time on the north face of Sierra Nevada.

Façade of Guadix Cathedral.

Cave neighbourhood in Guadix.

This street is typical of Salobreña.

Almuñécar. Playa del Tesorillo.

Next two pages, panoramic view of Moclín. ▶

The southern face of this important mountain chain shelters the exquisite region of Granada's Alpujarra, where Andalusia stretches up to heaven. Its untamed villages –**Trevélez, Capileira, Órgiva, Cádiar**–, the place of the Moriscos' last resistance before being expelled, have rows of white houses on terraces against the rugged geography, from where the sea can be seen. In just a few kilometres, the visitor goes down from the fine mountain air, the woods and the smell of wood fires to the cane plantations and beaches of **Motril, Salobreña** and **Almuñécar,** bathed in the Costa Tropical's mild climate. The province is yet again different in its western section, in the **Alhama** region, the city of the singers of Spanish romances, with its Arab baths, and in towns –**Moclín, Montefrío,** of daring adventures, and its main town, **Loja**– on the last border of the old kingdom of Granada.

Doñana National Park.
El Acebuche Reception Centre.

Dunes in Doñana National Park.

HUELVA

Coast, Condado, Tierra Llana, Andévalo and Sierra are the keys to the province of Huelva, which is the most westerly region of Andalusia and borders Portugal along the line of the River Guadiana. The regions are laid out as bands increasing in height from the coast inland, running from the Atlantic to the mountains of Sierra Morena. Each of these has different features and characters, even though they form one single region to the west of the River Guadalquivir valley.
The Costa de la Luz is made up of open beaches and sand formations in the shapes of dunes, bars, estuaries and wetlands, as can be seen in the **Doñana national park,** which is the symbol of the nature to be found in Huelva and one of the most important ecological reserves in Europe. Thousands of species of aquatic birds, many of which are of exceptional interest for

The lynx, the boar, the spoonbill and the flamingo are just four of the many different species that live in Doñana National Park.

Shrine of Our Lady of El Rocío.

their rarity, gather in their lagoons. Meanwhile the jewel of Spanish fauna, the lynx, stalks through the woods and scrub and is also the symbol of this unique refuge for the conservation of the continent's natural heritage. Next to the park is the milestone of popular culture in the form of the hermitage to Our Lady of El Rocío, whose famous Spring pilgrimage, the most popular in the region, attracts a huge crowd of pilgrims that follow the route between the pine trees and salt marshes to the sound of the flute and the small drum. The vineyards of El Condado stretch out from **El Rocío** and **Almonte,** with the centre of the wine region being **La Palma,** a village that produces generous wines, and inland **Niebla,** which nearly preserves intact its Medieval appearance, with a Roman bridge, castle and ringed by Arab walls in warm shades of ochre.

The important role played by Huelva in relation to America is focused on the estuaries of the Rivers Tinto and Odiel, on the Franciscan monastery of **La Rábida** where Christopher Colombus organised his first voyage, and on the town of **Palos de la Frontera,** from where his caravels set sail for America in 1492. The important step that opened the gates to the New World was taken from this area where Colombus lived and planned. The exquisite hamlet of **Moguer** recalls the universally known poet, Juan Ramón Jiménez.

The statue to Colombus, looking out over the ocean, and the Sanctuary of La Cinta, where the admiral went after finishing his voyage, mark the entrances to the city of Huelva, lying between the port on the banks of the River Odiel and a cornice. The abundance and quality of the discoveries that archaeology has come up with show the importance role that Huelva has had since Tartessian times,

Niebla. Above, courtyard in the Castle of Los Guzmán; below, Roman bridge over the River Tinto.

La Rábida. Above, Las Carabelas dock; below, Monastery of Santa María de La Rábida.

Moguer. Santa María de la Granada.

Moguer. Tile in memory of Juan Ramón Jiménez.

Tomb of the founder of the Convent of Santa Clara.

Moguer. Inside the Church of Santa Clara.

Huelva. Columbus Monument at La Punta del Sebo.

while the shipping of minerals, the English district and the notable list of modernist buildings spread out through the city are proof of the boom as a result of the mining operations run by British capital from the end of the 19th century. The coastal strip consisting of bright beaches stretches towards **Lepe** and its productive strawberry fields, before ending up in the ports of **Isla Cristina,** whose fish auction rooms have the best fish, and **Ayamonte,** where the River Guadiana that marks the frontier with Portugal flows into the sea.

The fields of Tierra Llana, **Gibraleón, Trigueros,** cover the land to the hills of Andévalo, a region of woods, meadows, mines and simple villages, and cradle of the fandango. **Valverde del Camino** and **Zalamea** are the traditional main centres, where leather is worked and eau-de-vie, produced, and **Riotinto** and **Nerva,** its mining centres, with impressive open excavations where the rich colour range of the bowels of the earth can be seen. The austere power of this vision changes in the upper part of the province. The **Sierra de Aracena** turns the land green again with the thick cover of woods, chestnut trees and holm oaks, which provide the acorns used to feed the herds of Iberian pigs that provide "pata negra" ham, the coverted speciality that has conquered the world's most exquisite planets. As excellent as the mountain gastronomy are the picturesque towns with white house and red roofs: **Aracena,** the capital of the mountain area, with a castle and a church that was build by the Templars on the top of a hill cut through by the Gruta de las Maravillas, incredible caves with lake, stalactites and stalagmites which perfectly fit in with the name, **Alájar,** lying in a valley at the foot of the rock to which Arias Montano, withdrew, **Jabugo,** the ham town par excellence, **Almonaster,** with a thousand-year old mosque, now a chapel, **Aroche,** on the Portuguese frontier and right in the heart of this natural park that makes up this wonderful mountain area.

Huelva. Above, Columbus's House and the Palacio de Congresos; left, outside view of the Cathedral; below, the English district.

Above, view of the port at Ayamonte; below, fisherman mending his nets.

Panoramic view of Martos nestled among olive groves.

JAEN

The Alto Guadalquivir basin lays out the paradise to be found inside Jaen, a surprising revelation where nature and the wealth of monuments reach levels that are difficult to beat. The considerable area of this region includes the top of the Betic valley bordered by Sierra Morena, the Cazorla, Segura and Las Villas mountain ranges, where the Gran Río bubbles up out of the earth, and the steep southern chain of Sierra Mágina. The olive tree, over a thousand years old and symbol of civilisation, dominates the landscape and feeds the pulse of the province: straight lines of olive trees cover the countryside, hillocks and slopes as far as the eye can see, and make it quite clear that it is the first oil-producing area in the world, whose production equals or is higher that any other country outside Spain.

The most widely-used road between the central plateau and Andalusia cross the Despeñaperros pass, which is the threshold to the Autonomous Region of Andalusia in the middle of Sierra Morena. The scale of its eroded forms still protect large areas in their original state, which are a delight for the senses –the natural parks of Andújar and Despeñaperros, the Cimbarra waterfalls–, as well as providing an excellent hunting area. Another feature well-worth a visit are the mountain villages, **La Carolina** and the set of Nuevas Poblaciones founded in the 18th century to colonise what was previously desert, **Bailén,** previously and still at the crossroads of several routes and scene of the first defeat of Napoleon's army, **Linares,** the important mining city, and **Andújar,** filled with magnificent architecture, whose pilgrimage of Our Lady of la Cabeza attracts the highest number of pilgrims in Upper Andalusia.

Quiet and hard-working villages are scattered amongst the hills and olive groves that cover the countryside and Jaen's Sierra Sur mountain range. Their foundations lie in a thousand-year old past that played its most important roles in the Iberian period and during the upheavals of the Reconquista, when Jaen was given the title of Santo Reino (Holy Kingdom), as it was the first region to beat the Muslims. The settlements, forts, castles, places, churches and other features of **Arjona, Porcuna,**

Next two pages, night-time view of Jaen Cathedral.

Jaen. Castle of Santa Catalina. ▶

General view of Alcalá la Real and La Mota Fortress.

Jaen. The Baths of Ali, in the basement of Villardompardo Palace.

Martos, Alcaudete, Alcalá la Real, and the capital itself, provide proof of this. It is hard to find another route with such historical density.

The city of **Jaen,** which in Arab means "caravan post", offers the visitor an attractive spot to stop at the foot of the haughty Santa Catalina's mount and its impregnable castle, which currently is a peaceful balcony offering marvellous views. *Aurgis* in the Iberian and Roman times, it flourished under its Muslim and Christian lords and enjoyed years of wealth after the Medieval conflicts were over. The Renaissance blended in well with Jaen's stone and the masterpiece of the **Cathedral** resulted from this harmony. An outstanding creation with an impressive façade embossed with sculptures and fine towers on the corners, the relics of the Santa Faz is worshipped inside alongside a valuable collection of artistic treasurers. The series of statutes and Iberian reliefs to be found in Jaen's Museum, which offers the best

display of its sophisticated culture, is equally worth mentioning. The delightful old districts, the Magdalena, San Juan,... bring together the old mosques, Arab baths, monasteries with the magic of the legends and the friendliness of the local people. The charm of the province once again works its magic at the city gates, when the visitor looks across to the Sierra Mágina range, a natural sanctuary surrounded by a halo of tales of miracles and important towns such as **Huelma** and **Jódar,** when the top-quality olive oil produced.
Further up the valley, two outstanding monuments stand on the slopes, where the Renaissance left its most important works with two classical gems of immeasurable value: **Baeza** and **Úbeda.** The squares of El Pópulo and Santa

Inside Baeza Cathedral. ▶

Baeza. Plaza del Pópulo.

Baeza. Plaza de Santa María.

Úbeda. Above, Plaza Vázquez de Molina and Church of El Salvador; below and right, a forge and a potter at work.

Castle built by the Knights Templar in La Iruela.

Panoramic view of Segura de la Sierra. ▶

María, the Cathedral, the Jabalquinto palace, the town halls adorn Baeza, the city that was praised by the poet, Antonio Machado. El Salvador, Santa María de los Reales Alcázares, the houses of Las Cadenas and Las Torres are only a hint of the never-ending list of harmonious building that made up the magnificent setting of Úbeda, which is considered to be the most representative town of Andalusian classicism. The display provided by the sources of the Guadalquivir is very different. All the force of nature can be seen in the **Cazorla, Segura** and **Las Villas** mountain ranges, and where the largest natural park in Andalusia and Spain is to be found. The olive trees are replaced by Holm oaks, pine trees and a wide range of upland vegetation and fauna, until the bare limestone peaks are reached. Interwoven with this huge geological twisted formation are stunning villages and hamlets, **Quesada, Hornos, Segura, La Iruela,** and **Cazorla,** the main mountain town, which clings to the side of the mountain under the keep of its castle.

A street corner in old Marbella town.

MALAGA

The typical Mediterranean blend of sea and mountains characterises the province of Malaga along its whole length from the Straits until it reaches the border with Granada. However, its fame is mainly due to its coastline, the famous Costa del Sol, which without doubt is the area of Andalusia that is best known through out the world. Along its western stretch, beach and coves, old fishing villages and country towns, modern hotel complexes, residential developments, marinas and golf courses stand side up side and make up a cosmopolitan area based on tourism and leisure. **Estepona, Fuengirola, Torremolinos** are on either side of **Marbella,** the nerve centre of this coast blessed with an extremely mild climate, with over 320 days of sunshine a year and an average temperature of 22 °C, which, if this was not enough, also enjoys clean water and enciting countryside closeby, such as the Bermeja and Blanca mountain ranges. It is not surprising that this area is chosen by holiday-makers from all over the world.

Marbella. Above, panoramic view with Puerto Banús and the Sierra Blanca; below, a mosque.

Panoramic night-time view of Malaga.

Inside the Alcazaba.

The city of Malaga stands at the mid-way point between the western and eastern sections of the Costa del Sol. The Phoenicians did not fail to notice this ideal situation and laid the foundations of *Malaka,* and the Romans and Muslims, who gave it its final recognition, were also aware of its importance. It was the Kingdom of Granada's trading centre, crowned by the Gibralfaro castle and the Alcazaba, half fort and half palace from where magnificent views of the city and port can be enjoyed. After being taken by the Catholic Monarchs, **Malaga** continued to be a busy trading centre. Its Cathedral, which is a mixture of Gothic, Renaissance and Baroque, known affectionately as "la manquita" (the little one-armed lady) as one of its towers was not finished, the Bishop's Palace, the Custom's house and other buildings in the old town provide proof of its past. The elegance of its eclectic architecture and its parks are evidence of the

Walls and towers of the Alcazaba, Malaga.

Above left, Malaga Cathedral; above right, Malaga Town Hall; left, church in Nerja.

prosperity that it enjoyed up to the start of the 20th century, thanks to the trading of wines, raisons and fruits. The outstanding painter of magnetising eyes, Pablo Picasso, was born and spent his early years here. Nowadays, Málaga, lively and bustling with activity as in its heyday, stretches along the valleys and up the slops and has nearly half a million inhabitants. Its traditional atmosphere can still be enjoyed in its wineries and beach-side restaurants where typical dishes and delicious fried fish are served. Another beautiful part of the coast stretches east to **Nerja,** a picturesque setting of beaches and cliffs, with the rich art heritage that covers the walls of its cave. The Axarquía region, where its Moorish roots are still very obvious, is inland from Nerja. Its capital, **Vélez Malaga,** is accompanied by a handful of white mountain villages –**Torrox, Frigiliana, Cómpeta**–, located high up on rocks and slopes between vines, almond and olive trees. The forest areas of Los

Inside the Cueva de Nerja.

Balcón de Europa, in Nerja.

Panoramic view of Cómpeta.

Bullfighting ring in Ronda.

Arab baths in Ronda.

Following page, the gorge and New Bridge, Ronda. ▶

Montes and the popular "ventas" (outdoor restaurants), where the "verdiales" groups (typical music from this area) meet, are also to be found there.

The wild uplands of the Serranía de Ronda form the inland backbone of the western part of the province. The romantic stereotype of Andalusia of brave smugglers and bull-fighters was crystallised here amongst crags, caves, gorges and villages that perch on the mountainsides like eagles' nests. The hidden town in the valleys of the River Genal prepare the way to the dream-like city: **Ronda,** set on the edge of a vertical gorge and a narrow pass through impressive walls broken up only by the New Bridge built in the 18th century. The gorge separates "The City", the original centre, elegant and walled, from the Mercadillo, the modern town. A mythical ring stands in the upper part: the La Maestranza bull-ring

of Rhonda, whose beauty lies in its austerely worked stone. A bullring that saw the birth of the art of modern-bullfighting thanks to the skill of the bullfighter, Pedro Romero.
The geological spectacle continues along the Las Nieves mountain range and its Spanish fir forests, until the stunning Los Gaintanes gorge, that the River Guadalhorce has formed opposite the town of **Ardales,** while the Torcal de Antequera offers the visitor's imagination the delights of the strange figures chizzeled in the rock. The region of **Antequera** and its plains bring us back to the Betic land. It is a city rich in history and archaeology age-old dolmens, Arab citadels, Renaissance churches and many other monuments, with other nearby attractions such as **Archidona** or the salt-water lake of Fuente de Piedra, home to the brightly-coloured flocks of pink flamingos.

▲ *Gateway into the Alcazaba, in Antequera.*

Torcal de Antequera. ▼

Antequera. Santa María Collegiate Church.

Night-time view of Seville, with the Guadalquivir and the Giralda.

SEVILLE

The largest city of Andalusia, the fourth in Spain in terms of population, stands on the banks of the River Guadalquivir, which, now much larger in its downstream course, cross right down the middle of the city. Seville is part of the select groups of cities that has been noted down beforehand in the schedule of every traveller, a "must" and the mere mention of its name triggers a torrent of recollections. Eternal, radiant, proud, filled with culture and monuments, it is the true personification of the South. On the one hand, it offers the mature fruit of the many civilisations that have settled in the region. On the other hard, it makes the most of the extroverted, passionate and hospitable nature of the people from the south.

According to myth, *Hispalis* was founded by Hercules when he came to the west to defeat Gerion and take his bulls. What is certain is that archaeological remains show that it existed at least from the 8th century BC, when the Tartessian settlement under the influence of Phonecians was founded. The Carambolo treasure, a fabulous collection of solid gold items, provides undeniable proof of its wealth and the presence of Italica, the fist Latin colony in the Peninsula, gives an idea of the importance of this area in Roman times. Under the Muslims, *Isbiliya,* in all its urban splendour was centred around the Giralda Tower. Even though another extraordinary chapter came later thanks to the discovery of America, as Seville was granted the monopoly on the traffic to the Indies. Called the great Babylonia of Spain and warehouse for the world's riches, the city of Seville, the home of Velázquez and Murillo, then knew its Golden Age. Based on this, and favoured by events such as the 1929 Ibero-American Exhibition and the 1992 World's Fair, Seville is entering the 21st century as one of the most beautiful and attractive cities that can be imagined.

Las Santas Justa y Rufina, painted by Murillo.

Reproduction of a famous hoard, the Tesoro del Carambolo.

La Giralda seen from calle Mateos Gago.

The old part of Seville, one of the largest in Europe, is filled with delightful and interesting places for the visitor to admire and visit. The emblematic bell-tower of the **Giralda** stands in the heart of area with most monuments and is the symbol of the union between Christian and Islamic art and the great **Cathedral** church, the third Catholic church in terms of sizes and a magnificent example of Gothic architecture together with a long repertoire of other styles, whose artistic content rivals the best museums. The fascinating atmosphere provided by the **Reales Alcázares** has been nurtured over the centuries. Its huge grounds bring together the mastery of the Muslim and Mudejar craftsmen who worked on Pedro I's palace and the skills of the stonemasons and landscapers who built the Gothic Palace and the idylic gardens. The Archive of the Indias, where the records on the New World are kept, the Casa de la Moneda, the coffers of its precious metal, the Hospital of La Caridad, a Baroque gem thanks to its architecture and painting and the Torre de Oro, the watchtower that looked over the old

Above, the Royal Chapel, with the tombs of Alfonso X, known as Alfonso the Wise, and his wife; right, altarpiece at the Cathedral's main altar; below, outside view of Seville Cathedral.

Almohad walls and the Alcázar Gardens; below, on the right, the Mercury Fountain.

port, are testimony to the wealth of American Seville, while the Maestranza bullring's fine building acts as the bullfighting seat of learning in the region where it is most ingrained.
The narrow alleyways of the Barrio de Santa Cruz merge into the labyrinth that makes up the heart of Seville. Here, the visitor will come across a small square with a wrought cross or the statue of Don Juan, against the backdrop of his adventures, between palm trees, orange trees and the fragrance of orange blossom. winding streets with poetic names –Pepper, Water, Air, Life road– and delightful bars that are the ideal spot to have a drink and a tapa, the small

Torre del Oro.

Hospital of la Caridad.

The Prince's Gate, at the Maestranza Bullring.

Cruz de la Cerrajería in the Plaza de Santa Cruz.

Courtyard in the Casa de Pilatos. ▶

portions that allow the visitor to discover the tasty local gastronomy.
A series of equally delightful spots is dotted around the old town: the luxurious mansion of the Casa de Pilatos, the plateresque Town Hall and calle Sierpes, the winding road that is the main road of the famous Semana Santa (Holy Week), the Fine Arts Museum, the second art collection in Spain with an outstanding collection of the Baroque school, together with many churches and convents and, of course, the popular districts, that stretch towards the Alameda de Hércules and the Macarena, the church dedicated to the most popular Virgin that is situated by the Arab walls and the seat of the Andalusian parliament.
The many-sided latticework of Seville even stretches to the other bank of the river, through

Alameda de Hércules, with its Sunday street market.

Above, the pilgrimage to El Rocío: the path as it crosses the city and the crossroads at El Quema; below, the Feria de Abril: booths, horses and Gypsy outfits.

Above, main façade of San Telmo Palace; below, the old Tobacco Factory, now the University.

Triana, a district filled with local colour, ceramic workshops and the sound of Flamenco, through the grounds of the *Feria de Abril* (April Fair) and through the Cartuja, a mixture of the past and daring modernity that materialised in 92. The sloping rods of the Alamillo bridge today symbolises the image of the contemporary city. In the wider area to the south, the romantic shady Maria Luisa Park surround the San Telmo Palace, the Tobacco Factory, linked to the myth of Carmen the cigar maker and the Plaza de España, an unusual hemicycle of bricks and tiles flanked by two pointed towers.
The capital is surrounded by the largest province, which is also one of the flatest and

Tile work at the Plaza de España.

View of the Plaza de España.

The ruins of Italica speak of its glorious past.

Above. Cazalla de la Sierra; below, meadows along the Sierra Norte, Seville.

fertile in Andalusia. There are the olive groves of El Aljarafe, next to the ruins of Italica which are proof of the Roman inheritance. The most rugged landscape is in the Sierra Norte, the natural park made up of mountains and meadows that surrounds **Cazalla.** La Campiña accounts for the largest areas, with sizeable white towns with important monuments. **Carmona,** an unspoilt jewel, **Écija,** the city of the sun, the elegant **Osuna, Marchena, Estepa, Morón, Utrera, Lebrija...** make up a truly captivating picture. Finally, the sea breezes from the Atlantic can be felt along the course of the Bajo Guadalquivir and paddy fields and salt marshes stretch towards the open horizon and become one with the Doñana park.

Torre de San Juan, Écija.

Osuna. Façade of the Council Tithe Barn.